Contents

for Carolyn, Naomi and Calum

Welcome

Here at The Chandlery our constant quest is to surprise and charm our diners with a tantalising combination of tradition, bold invention and the freshest produce in the northern hemisphere. I have great pleasure in sharing with you some of my favourite recipes that have delighted the gourmet palates of our international clientele. I hope you enjoy them and I look forward to sharing the unique Skye experience in the near future.

The Bosville

The Bosville in Portree was established in 1965 and forms the nucleus of fast-growing Macleod Hotels UK Ltd. Good food defines our company, as The Chandlery demonstrates. Our recent acquisitions, the Broadford Hotel and Portree House, will set similarly high culinary standards. Both are magnificent properties and the Broadford, dating back to 1611, is where the famous Drambuie liqueur was first produced. Its secret recipe was bequeathed to the Mackinnon family by Bonnie Prince Charlie after the '45 Jacobite rebellion.

A refined palate

John Kelly's life-long love for food has found its perfect expression at The Chandlery

John Kelly was always fascinated by food and his earliest culinary memories are of his mother's mouth-watering traditional Scottish mutton broths, millionaires shortbread and baking. As a child in the highland port of Oban, he loved going fishing. "I used to go up to Loch Etive with my mother and father, catch trout and cook them in butter over a small fire in tin foil with a few potatoes," he says.

His passion for producing beautifully and sensitively crafted food is as strong today as it was when he first went to college in Inverness to pursue his ambition to be a chef. While some consider cuisine as a career move, for John it was a natural vocation. Blessed with an exceptionally delicate and intelligent palate, he can identify the ingredients in a dish with a forensic accuracy that is stunning.

But as the many regular aficionados of the Chandlery will testify, he is a charismatic host for whom feedback from guests in his restaurant is extremely important. Even changes in the weather

feed his need to experiment with the fresh produce available to him on the Island.

But John's effortless improvisation with ingredients comes from his disciplined early training in the classic French methods of making soups, sauces and stocks - the vital basic skills then leave you free to experiment. After graduation he was hungry for any kind of experience that would give him new ideas and expose him to the country's brightest and best chefs. "I remember calling the Peat Inn and asking to work for the day for free, just to gain experience. It was worth it," he says.

But it was in the mid-80s while working in Aberdeen's top restaurant under a French chef that John really came into his own. It proved to be his own Kitchen Confidential moment...complete with piping bags of pureed potatoes flying past his ear on several occasions.

"It was the first kitchen I had worked in where people were truly passionate about food," he says. "This was 20 years ago, doing absolute classics like frogs' legs, snails, cassoulet and tarte au citron, all in French style. It was an invaluable lesson in learning how to maintain consistency."

The temperamental chef worked the classic Escoffier system during service. All food would be brought to him, he would check it, taste it and only if it was good enough would he finish it off and allow it to go through the pass. If it wasn't up to his exacting standards, explains John, "he would say 'non' and you would be sent back to cook it again".

But the temper tantrums and histrionics that characterise the kitchens of many celebrity chefs are absent from the smoothly run Chandlery. His team know that one steely look from John means that normal calm must be restored. The only thing that simmers or boils in John's kitchen is the food.

By 1993, following promotions to various renowned establishments around the country John wanted a new challenge. "I was 26 and desperate to have a restaurant of my own. I knew the type of food I wanted to offer and if I got a restaurant of my own, then I knew that I could do it." He took on a small place near Stirling called Farriers, followed four years later by his successful tenure of a restaurant on Arran.

By 2000 he was ready to move on again, still on a quest for greater control over the restaurant. He got a call from the Bosville Hotel. It was not a difficult decision. "The island was already building a reputation as a good food location. Then I talked to the owner and it seemed to be a place that had real ambitions as a destination for cuisine. The Bosville didn't just want their menus tweaked - they wanted me to push the quality of the cooking as far as I could."

They had found the right man. John is considered to have forged the art and science of cuisine into something more akin to alchemy. After a long day cooking at the Chandlery, John can often be found alone in the kitchen experimenting with

" *After a night's service, you realise there is no better job in the world*

new flavours, ingredients and recipe ideas.

With two children, John and his wife Carolyn were attracted to Skye by the opportunity it offered for a typical island life, living in a small community with a safer environment.

What makes John unique is that, unlike celebrity chefs who famously never touch a kitchen knife once they have taken off their whites, he likes to cook at home. It gives him another environment in which to experiment. "They are now getting into shellfish," he says proudly of his children. However, he ruefully confesses that he was more popular when he brought home all of the desserts for the new menu to test on the family.

Even now, John can still be found sipping his favourite double espresso and smoking a cigar as he ponders the question of what it takes to be a chef.

"It is a tough profession. The hours are long and you can get very tired. Unless you enjoy it and love food then you are going to get fed up quite quickly."

However, he has a ready answer for his own question: "After a night's service, you realise there is no better job in the world."

Sun, sea and Skye

The island's appetising harvest is fresh, abundant and distinctive

It was the quest for perfection in the quality of produce that first drew John Kelly to Skye. Whereas a decade ago the island's world-renowned seafood was all being sent abroad to satisfy gourmet palates in foreign climes, the Chandlery now has the pick of the catch.

"A huge amount has been done to publicise the island and people now know it as a culinary destination," says John. The introduction of an innovative food distribution chain on the island has vastly increased the amount of local produce staying on Skye.

Access to such special local ingredients enables John to create dishes that reflect his love of French regional cuisine. "There the countryside produces a type of food and only then do the chefs make the recipes. I have tried to base my cookery on exactly the same philosophy," he says.

The island's reputation for seafood is the main attraction for discerning food lovers from the UK and overseas. John is shamelessly partisan in this regard. "My favourite ingredients are langoustines and scallops – basically any kind of fish"

He starts to reel off recipes. "You

The view of Portree
from The Chandlery

Scallops from
Oakes Marine

" *The island's reputation for seafood is the main attraction for discerning food lovers*

can't beat Skye mussels," he says with undisguised passion.

The mussels he uses from Loch Eishort are the best in the world. The hint of fresh water that has washed through the island's peat make them enviably sweeter than those that grow anywhere else on the planet.

"It is a dish you know is going to be good when you cook it. Garlic and white wine works so well with shellfish".

Framed by Idrigill Point and the sea stacks of Macleod's Maidens to the west and Rubha nan Clach to the east, Loch Bracadale nurtures the crabs that end up in John's kitchen.

So high is the quality that John believes that the natural delicacy of the crustacean is sufficient.

"I don't want to cook the crab, you have to eat it as it comes in," he says, adding that all the dish requires is a little seasoning and some crème fraiche. "It

has a wonderful, huge flavour".

But there is a special place in John's heart for langoustines. "These ingredients are so good on their own," he says.

Local fisherman Donald "Ginger" Gillies brings langoustines to the restaurant every day. He goes out at 7am and comes back at 5pm bringing John a creel. "We telephone him on his mobile telephone to check what time," says Kelly. "Sometimes he is in range, sometimes not, but if he has a missed call he knows that it is us."

As he races up the hill to the Chandlery to make service, Ginger knows he is delivering what must be the freshest langoustines in Britain.

In many ways, langoustines reflect the gastronomic change that has come over the island in the last decade. It used to be that the entire catch was crated up for export to haute cuisine establishments in France and Spain.

Now, however, Skye langoustines have become so prevalent on the island that they are almost a currency. "If someone does a job for you they get a bag of langoustines in return," says John. "Then I often get a call asking how to cook them."

He is reviving the time-honoured techniques for preparing the shellfish. Only now, he explains, are we getting into the way of cooking a batch whole and putting them in the middle of the table.

"I remember doing that for my children when they were younger," he recalls with a smile.

"I cooked the langoustines, peeled them and used the shells to make a bisque. Then I put the soup on table, a pile of langoustines, fresh bread and salad for their tea."

Fresh, abundant and distinctive. Skye's appetising harvest from land and sea exerts an irresistible pull on chefs and epicureans alike.

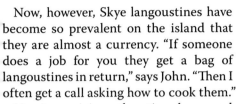

Shitake mushrooms from Lusta Fungi

Basil from Glendale Salads

The fine art

The Chandlery surprises and charms with a unique combination of tradition and bold invention

While other chefs scour the planet in search of ever-more exotic ingredients, John Kelly takes a different approach. "I get my inspiration from the produce," he says simply.

To an outsider, putting a menu together can seem to be an arcane practice. However, John takes a more direct approach. He creates dishes with what appears on his doorstep.

"One of my suppliers will bring something in and ask, 'This is what we have, can you do something with it?'" It is a challenge he relishes, rather than a penance or a conundrum.

While ingredients provide the initial muse, the art of combining them can be influenced by anything from Proustian recollection to trial-and-error.

"When you see the Loch Eishort oysters you have to ask yourself how best to bring out their flavour," he says. "I remember

of the menu

eating melon and oysters together many years ago. The flavours just matched and I wanted something – rather summery – to give a freshness to it."

The evolution of a dish is sometimes a long process. "It can take a while," John admits. A dish can appear on the menu and then be refined until it achieves perfection.

He and his colleagues are obsessive about feedback. Every night in the Chandlery restaurant John enjoys talking to customers about what works, and very rarely, what doesn't.

It can be difficult at times to second-guess what people like. He mentions the Earth and Sea Salad. "People keep asking for it," he says of the dish that combines earthy beetroot, sea-scented langoustines and pigeon breast.

John sees Skye's remoteness as an advantage that feeds his creativity. "I want to do regional cooking – using what we can get here," he says.

Trendy, fusion food is frankly too faddy. "I can't see us serving oysters with soy and wasabi here. It doesn't sound right," he says.

"We make French-influenced Scottish food. All I aim to do is to bring out the superb qualities of the produce to maximum effect."

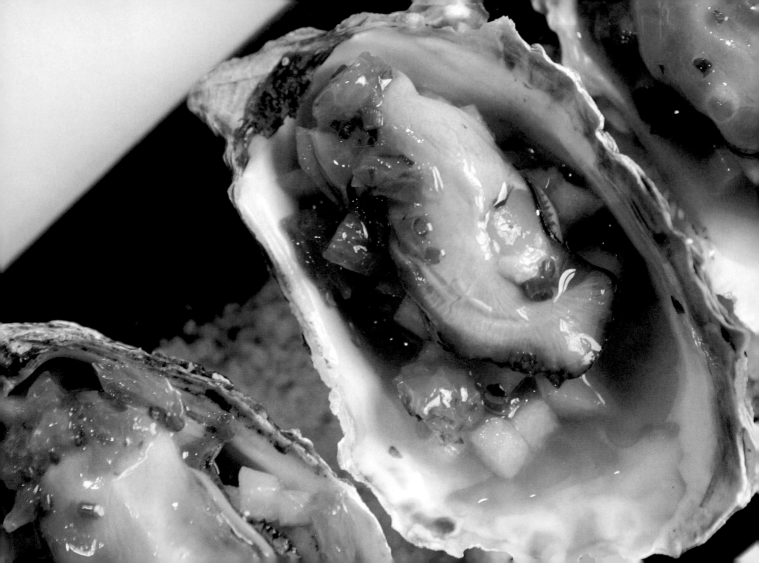

Loch Eishort oysters with melon
and pink grapefruit dressing

Hors d'oeuvres

Bracadale crab with tomato salad and mustard vinaigrette

Serves 4

Ingredients

6 plum tomatoes
1 teaspoon of chopped chives
8 oz white crab meat
2 spring onions (chopped)
4 tbsp crème fraiche
2 floz white wine vinegar
1 tbsp grain mustard
½ tsp English mustard
6 floz olive oil
3 oz salad leaves
Dash of extra virgin oil
Salt and pepper

Method

For the tomato salad, skin, de-seed and then chop the tomatoes into small cubes, season and add a dash of extra virgin olive oil and the chives.

Mix the crab meat with the crème fraiche and spring onions and season.

To make the vinaigrette, whisk the vinegar and mustards together then pour in the olive oil slowly while whisking. Season with salt and pepper.

To assemble

Take four cold plates and place a salad ring in the middle. Layer with the tomatoes on the bottom, then the crab mix and salad leaves tossed in vinaigrette on top. Remove the salad ring, spoon the vinaigrette around the salad and then serve.

"Try and buy fresh crabs as frozen or tinned crabs simply do not have the same flavour."

Cured mutton with lentil emulsion and potato salad

Serves 4

Ingredients
Gigot of mutton (cured and cooked)
3 oz salad leaves
3 oz red lentils
1 oz basic vinaigrette
2 floz olive oil (good quality)
2 large potatoes
2 tablespoons crème fraiche
1 shallot diced
Salt and pepper
Bay leaf
Sprig of thyme
Tablespoon chives chopped

"In this recipe it is probably easier to buy a gigot of mutton and use the rest of the meat in other recipes. We use mutton that has been salt cured for two weeks. Then we poach it for 2 hours in water with bay leaf peppercorns and thyme. Keep the cooking stock for the lentils."

For the mutton
Bring to boil the pint of mutton cooking stock, add the lentils, bay leaf and thyme and poach until the lentils start to break down. Pour into a sieve and leave to strain for 10 minutes. The lentils will start to dry out. When the lentils are almost cool pick out the bay leaf and thyme and pour into a food processor. Switch on and pour in the olive oil slowly. Season the lentils mixture and reserve.

For the potato salad
Peel and dice the potato and boil until firm but cooked, strain and leave to dry and cool. Place the potatoes in a bowl, add the chives, crème fraiche and shallot mix and season.

To arrange
For this dish, we use metal cake cutters to put the potato salad in to get a nice shape. Slice the mutton very thinly and arrange them overlapping on the plate, arrange the potato salad on each plate.

Mix the salad leaves with the vinaigrette and place on top of the potato salad. For the lentils you can just spoon onto the plate or if you have a piping bag you can pipe a line round the lentils.

To finish
Drizzle a little olive oil on the mutton and give the dish a few turns of ground pepper.

Herring and potato terrine with cream and smoked paprika dressing

Serves 8

Ingredients
8 fillets of herring
6 large potatoes
2 leaves of gelatine
1 floz white wine
2 tbsp thinly sliced spring
onions
Small bunch of flat parsley
Salt and cracked peppercorns
3 tbsp water

Dressing:
1 shallot, finely chopped
crème fraiche
Juice of a lemon
1 tsp smoked paprika
Salt and cracked peppercorns
6 floz crème fraiche

"Test the terrine with a thin sharp knife to make sure the potatoes are cooked."

Method
Line a terrine mould with cling film. Soak the gelatine in water until soft. Wash and peel the potatoes.

Chop the parsley and mix with the spring onions. Slice the potatoes to quarter of an inch deep and the same width as the terrine.

Layer the potatoes on the bottom of the terrine and sprinkle with the herbs and season with salt and peppercorns. Place some herring on top and then alternate until there are 4 layers of herring, then top with potatoes.

Warm the white wine and melt the gelatine in it. Pour over the terrine. Cover with tin foil and bake in a bain marie for 1 hour in a preheated oven at gas mark 5 (190°C).

When ready, test with a knife, cool and place a weight on top - press for 24 hours in the fridge.

For the dressing
Mix the crème fraiche with the shallot and the paprika and season.

To assemble
Slice the terrine and place in the middle of the plate then drizzle the crème fraiche mixture around the terrine.

Loch Eishort oysters with melon and pink grapefruit dressing

Serves 4

Ingredients
½ Charrantais melon
16 oysters
1 tbsp chopped coriander
Double measure sherry vinegar
⅓ pint of olive oil
1 pink grapefruit

Method
Take the melon, de-seed and dice into small cubes and mix with the coriander. Segment the grapefruit, avoiding any pith, over a bowl to catch the juice. Cut the grapefruit into small slices.

Open the oysters using an oyster knife, wrap your knife hand in a clean kitchen towel, then place each oyster onto rolled up kitchen towel. Work the knife into the pointed end of the oyster until the hinge breaks and then release the oyster with the knife. Place the oysters and the juice in a bowl, making sure there are no bits of shell. Reserve 16 deep shells and clean.

Sieve the oyster juice through a cloth into a pan and poach the oysters in the juice until firm. Take them out and keep warm. Add the grapefruit juice to the pan and reduce until there is 2 tablespoons of liquid left.

Place in a bowl and add the sherry vinegar. Whisk in the oil, add the grapefruit segments and season. Take the shells and place the melon on the bottom of each. Serve 4 oysters per person on top of the melon in the shells.

"Steaming the oysters means that they will open quite easily. If you want to serve them raw, invest in an oyster knife – this is the safest way to open them."

Donald 'Ginger' Gillies

MV The Golden Rule

"It is said that west coast prawns are the best you'll eat – and I believe that," says Donald 'Ginger' Gillies. He should know. A fisherman since the 60s, he has been working the prawn creels for the last eight years.

He used to trawl for langoustines, but believes you get a better quality of prawn from creels. "They are bigger and better, full of life," he says.

Every day, from May to December, Donald hauls 700-800 of the 1,500 pots he owns. "We then tube our prawns," he says. Each prawn is individually selected, put into its own compartment in a carton – the aforementioned tube – and then immersed in salt water so that they stay alive until he comes ashore at 5pm.

Although much of his catch is bought by Spanish and French buyers and carried on to waiting aeroplanes at Inverness, John Kelly probably gets the freshest langoustines in Britain. From Donald coming ashore to serving at the table in the Chandlery takes less than an hour.

Loch Sligachan hand dived scallops, pea shoots, artichoke and black pudding salad

Serves 4

Ingredients

12 large scallops trimmed
4 oz pea shoots
24 cherry tomatoes
1 small bunch of basil
3 floz olive oil
2 floz balsamic vinegar
1 shallot finely diced
Salt and pepper
2 oz black pudding
1 floz basic vinaigrette
2 cooked artichoke bottoms

Method

Wash the cherry tomatoes, dry and place onto a roasting tray. Drizzle with the balsamic vinegar. Place under a hot grill until soft. Allow to cool and then blitz in a blender. Chop the basil and add to the vinaigrette then whisk in 2floz of the olive oil and reserve.

Wash the pea shoots, pat dry and keep in the fridge. Dice the black pudding, slice the artichokes and pan fry in a little of the remaining olive oil.

Sear the scallops in the remaining olive oil, 1 minute on each side depending on the thickness of the scallop.

Place three scallops in the middle of each plate. Toss the pea shoots in a bowl with the basic vinaigrette, the black pudding and the artichokes and divide between the four plates. Surround with the cherry tomato vinaigrette.

"It is best to use hand dived scallops as dredged scallops will contain sand."

Pigeon and langoustine salad with beetroot crème fraiche

Serves 4

Ingredients
4 pigeon breast
12 langoustines
4 oz leek, carrot and
courgette in thin strips
¼ pint of basic vinaigrette
3 oz Glendale mixed salad
leaves
2 beetroot (cooked but firm)
6 tbsp crème fraiche
Salt and pepper
2 tbsp red wine vinegar

For the crème fraiche
Dice 1 beetroot. Add the red wine vinegar, stir in the crème fraiche and season with salt and pepper and reserve.

Blanch the langoustines in boiling water, cool and shell.

Then blanche the vegetable strips, cool and add the remaining beetroot cut into strips and reserve. Sautée the pigeon breast in a little olive oil and keep warm.

To assemble
Place a spoonful of beetroot crème fraiche in the middle of the plate. Place a salad ring on top. Toss the vegetable strips in vinaigrette, and place into the rings.

Lay 3 langoustines on top of vegetables. Slice the pigeon and arrange on top of the langoustines. Toss the salad in a little vinaigrette and arrange on top of the pigeon and serve.

"Use fresh beetroot, just peel and simmer in water. It is best to use gloves when peeling as it is difficult to get the juice off your hands."

Poached smoked salmon ravioli with baby leeks

Serves 4

Ingredients
10 oz piece of smoked salmon
4 oz diced baby leeks washed
4 tbsp cream
1 oz butter
Dash of herb oil (chive)
Dash of reduced balsamic
vinegar
3 oz fresh herb pasta

For the pasta
Roll out the pasta in a pasta machine to the thinnest setting. Cut 16 2inch squares and blanch.

For the leeks
Melt the butter in a pan and sweat the leeks (without colouring) and the cream. Reduce until it forms a sauce consistency and season. Keep warm.

For the salmon
Put a large pan of water on and bring to boil. Cut the salmon into 8 cubes and place into the water. Simmer for 1 minute.

To assemble
Decorate the plates with a ring of herb oil and balsamic vinegar. Add the pasta to simmering water and then drain into a colander. Assemble by placing the pasta in the centre, then a spoon full of leek mix, then the salmon – then repeat and put another square of pasta on top. Garnish with fresh herbs or deep fried leek strips.

"Making your own pasta looks difficult, but it is not a recipe that can go wrong. It is quick and easy and the difference in taste is huge."

Pressed ham hock and Portree landed langoustines terrine with puy lentil salad and truffle oil

Serves 8

Ingredients
2 ham hocks (smoked)
16 langoustines
½ lb Argyll ham
2 leaves gelatine
2 oz puy lentils (cooked)
3 oz salad leaves
4 pints water
Truffle oil
Bunch of chervil chopped
Herb oil

"The inspiration here is the old Scottish recipe for ham and haddie, poached haddock fillet and bacon. I put it on our very first menu and we did it for a long time with smoked, undyed haddock. I then tried it with monkfish and eventually came to langoustine."

Method
Poach ham hocks for 3 hours in the water. Remove from the pan and let it cool. Reserve 10 floz of the cooking liquid. Strip the meat from the bones and remove the fat and skin.

Soak the gelatine for 10 minutes in water. Bring the cooking ham hock liquid to the boil and add the gelatine. Take off the stove and cool, but do not allow it to set. Blanch the langoustines in boiling water and shell.

Line a terrine dish with cling film and then line with the smoked Argyll ham, overlapping the sides. Place a layer of the ham hock in the terrine then sprinkle with herbs. On top of the ham hock, place a layer of langoustines, then the herbs and then the ham again. At this point add the stock. Finish the top with a layer of Argyll ham and place a weight on top. Leave to set for 24 hours.

To serve
Remove the terrine from the mould and slice. Place in the middle of each plate. Toss the salad leaves in herb oil and arrange on the plates. Toss the puy lentils in herb oil. Check the seasoning and arrange the lentils in a circle around the terrine. Drizzle truffle oil onto the terrine. This is delicious served with homemade peach or apple chutney.

Rick Simons

Bracadale Crab

Originally from Newcastle, Rick Simons came to Skye 25 years ago. After stints as a paramedic, working on the oilrigs and then with the Northern Lighthouse Board, he became interested in crabs. "It was the right thing at the right time," he says. Now his hand-picked crab meat is eaten in quality dining rooms from Skibo Castle to Balmoral.

He genuinely loves his job. "You need to be brain dead to do this, so I am qualified," he says with a laugh. Simons has been investigating new technology such as blast freezing to offer the business more stability, but he is happy just the way he is now.

In the exceptionally clear waters of Skye there is such an abundance of crabs that "they need to be fished for management," says Simons. He washes them, kills them, cooks them, washes them again and with his team of three, breaks them apart and takes out the meat.

"There is a difference to doing it by hand," he says, saying that it simply tastes better, adding happily that his most high-tech piece of equipment to date is a spoon.

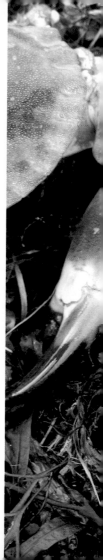

Hand dived scallop and celeriac lasagne

Serves 4

Ingredients

8 large scallops
10 floz fish stock
½ celeriac
5 floz white wine
1 oz grated parmesan
4 floz cream
8 oz washed spinach
2 tbsp chopped chives
2 oz butter
1 thumb of fresh ginger
1 shallot finely diced
Pinch of saffron strands

Method

To make the sauce peel and grate the ginger. In a pan melt 1oz butter. Add the shallot and ginger and sweat without colouring. Add the wine and fish stock, reduce by half, add the cream and reduce further until syrupy consistency is achieved. Seive and then add chives.

Take the celeriac and slice thinly. You will need 12 rectangle shapes large enough to hold two scallops. Bring a small pan of water to the boil and add the saffron and a pinch of salt. Poach the celeriac until soft. Remove and keep warm.

Wilt the spinach in the remaining butter and season. Cut the scallops in half and sear, taking care not to overcook.

Place 4 celeriac rectangles on a tray. Top with spinach and 2 half scallops, then pile up celeriac, spinach and scallops again – ending with celeriac. Sprinkle with parmesan and finish under a hot grill until glazed.

Place each lasagne on the middle of the plate and surround with sauce.

Skye fish soup
Serves 6

Ingredients
3 lb mixed fish (trimming, shells from langoustines, lobsters etc) cut into chunks
1 lb mussels and clams (blanched and shelled)
1 lb diced vegetables (carrot, onion, celery, fennel & leek)
8 cloves of garlic
1lb quartered tomatoes
6 tbsp tomato puree
1 pint dry white wine
Measure of pernod
Measure of brandy
pinch saffron strands
3½ pints water
4 floz olive oil
8 oz potatoes (peeled and sliced)
2 tbsp flour
1 tbsp dill chopped

"You can get everything ready, let it simmer and have a bowl for lunch, or two bowls for your tea with crusty bread! Any mixed fish will do for this recipe, apart from oily fish."

Method
Heat olive oil in a large pan. Add fish and vegetables and lightly brown. Add the flour, then the tomato purèe, tomatoes, potatoes, wine, brandy, pernod and water.

Bring to the boil and simmer for 1 hour. When ready, liquidise roughly with a hand held blender and pass through a fine sieve. Steam the mussels and clams until they open, then shell and reserve the meat.

Bring the soup back up to simmer and add the shell fish and the dill. Heat through and finish with cream and chives.

Warm lobster mousse, wilted spinach and keta sauce

Serves 4

Ingredients

8 oz raw lobster meat
2 egg whites
7 floz double cream
Salt and pepper
12 oz spinach (washed)
1 oz butter
10 floz fish stock
5 floz white wine
4 floz cream
2 tbsp chopped chives
2 tbsp keta (salmon eggs)

Method

Heat oven to gas mark 4 (180°C). Blanch the lobster first to get the meat. Drop the lobster into fast boiling water for 10 seconds then plunge into cold water. Once cool, shell all the meat. Place the meat in a food processor and switch on. Add the egg white a little at a time and then chill for ½ an hour, then add the cream again a little at a time and season.

To make the sauce

Reduce the fish stock and the wine by half, add the cream and reduce further until a light syrupy consistency is achieved, add the keta and the chives, keep warm.

To bake the mousse

Butter 4 ramekins and divide the lobster into them, bake in a hot water bain marie for 8 minutes. Wilt the spinach in the butter and season. Spinach will only take minutes in the hot butter.

To finish

Divide the spinach between 4 warm plates, turn out the lobster mousse, being careful as they will be hot. Place on the spinach and then spoon the sauce around the spinach.

"Keta is the name given to salted salmon eggs and can be found in most good delis."

44

West coast fish stew

Serves 4

Ingredients

12 langoustines
1 lb fresh mussels
1 lb clams
8 scallops
8 oz salmon
2 tbsp chopped chives
6 floz white wine
6 floz noilly prat
½ pt fish stock
½ pt double cream
Salt and pepper

Method

Blanch the langoustines in boiling water and then shell. Take the vein that runs down the back out and reserve the tails. Clean the mussels and clams, put them into a large pan and steam with the wine and noilly prat. Once opened, strain in a colander and reserve the juice. Keep 12 mussels and 8 clams for garnish and shell the rest.

Pour the cooking juice through a muslin cloth and return to the pan, reduce by half, then add the cream and the fish stock and then further reduce until a light syrupy consistency is achieved. Then season.

Slice the scallops in half, cut the salmon into eight pieces and add the salmon to the simmering sauce. Cook for 1 minute then add the scallops, langoustines, mussels and clams. Then sprinkle the chives into the sauce, simmer for a further minute until warmed through. Divide between 4 warm bowls, garnish with the reserved mussels and clams and serve with warm crusty bread.

"This is my own personal favourite kind of shellfish but you can substitute any others, depending on personal taste."

46

White bean soup with langoustines

Serves 4 – 6

Ingredients

Stock
10 live langoustines
1 clove of garlic
1 carrot diced
1 stalk of celery diced
1 onion diced
1 oz leeks diced
Measure of brandy
4 floz white wine
4 pints water
1 tbsp olive oil
Sprig of thyme and parsley

½ lb white beans (soaked overnight)
3½ floz double cream, salt, pepper and chives
1 small white onion diced
2 oz white of leek diced

"Always use live langoustines. Use any type of bean you prefer for this recipe."

For the stock
Blanch the langoustines, then shell, reserve the tails, shells and eggs if any.

In a large pan, heat the oil, add the shells and all the vegetables. Add the brandy, flame, and add the wine, water, herbs, peppercorn, garlic clove. Simmer for 40 minutes and then strain the stock.

For the soup
Sweat the onions and leeks, and then add the stock and beans. Simmer for 45 minutes or until the beans are soft. Finish with cream then liquidise and check the seasoning.

Keep four large langoustine tails as a garnish and chop the rest into chunks and warm through in the soup. Froth the soup with a hand blender and then pour into bowls. Garnish with the langoustines and chopped chives.

This soup is nice finished with a little olive oil, flavoured with chives or basil and garnished with the langoustine eggs.

Entrées

Fillet of Scottish beef oxtail bridie,
with a herbed skirlie crust, red cuillin
jus and shitake mushrooms

Duck with peppered turnips, blueberry sauce and roast sweet potatoes

Serves 4

Ingredients

4 6oz duck breasts
2 sweet potatoes
1 tbsp duck fat
10 oz turnips
2 oz butter
10 floz red wine
1 tsp cornflour
1 tbsp water
5 shallots (finely chopped)
4 floz port
8 floz stock (good chicken meat or game stock)
1 tbsp honey
6 tbsp blueberries
16 baby white turnips
6 floz water
2 oz butter
1 tsp chopped, flat parsley
1 floz olive oil
White pepper and salt
Piece of orange peel

"Remember, you have to keep the breast of duck pink. As soon as you overcook it, it becomes tough."

For the turnips

Place the peeled and cubed turnips in a large saucepan. Cover with water and simmer until soft (about 30 minutes), drain and leave to dry. Whilst still hot, mash with 2oz butter, white pepper and salt to taste.

For the blueberry sauce

Heat the olive oil and add the shallots, sweat for 1 minute, then add the port and stock, wine and honey then rapidly boil until the liquid is reduced by half.

Strain, add the blueberries and simmer for 3 minutes. Mix the cornflour with 1tbsp water in a bowl, and add to the sauce – which will thicken slightly. Reserve this sauce for later.

For the sweet potatoes

Peel and cut the sweet potatoes into small cubes, heat the duck fat and, when hot, add the potato. Season the potatoes and turn them in the duck fat until completely coated. Place in a medium hot oven gas mark 4 (180°C) for 30 minutes. Drain on kitchen paper when cooked and keep hot.

For the baby turnips

Bring 6fl oz water to the boil, add the baby turnips and the butter. Boil until the water has evaporated and the turnips are cooked, then toss in the parsley and keep warm.

Score the duck skin and pan fry the fillets in a hot pan, skin side down first, cooking until they are medium rare.

To arrange

Divide the mashed turnip between 4 warm plates, slice the duck and place on top. Surround with the blueberry sauce and garnish with the sweet potato and the baby turnips.

Fillet of Scottish beef oxtail bridie

Serves 4

Ingredients

4 6oz fillet steaks
3 oz oatmeal
4 shallots chopped finely
1 egg yolk
1 floz olive oil
2 oz beef dripping
1 egg beaten
2 lb oxtails, cut in to chunks
2 carrots
1 large onion
2 sticks celery
4 oz good puff pastry
¼ pt good ale
8 pints water
½ pt red wine
4 oz chopped shitake
mushrooms
Salt & pepper
1 white of leek
1 tbsp fresh tarragon chopped

*"Ask your butcher to cut
the oxtail in to chunks."*

Method

First roughly chop the carrot, leek, onion and celery and roast till browned with the oxtail chunks, then place in a large pan and cover with the water.

Deglaze the roasting tray with red wine and add to the pan. Bring to the boil and simmer for 3 hours, skimming regularly. Remove the oxtail from the stock and cool. Reserve the strained stock.

When the oxtail is cool enough to handle, remove the meat from the bone and dice. Take two shallots and finely dice. Sweat them in a little oil, then add the tarragon and cool. Once cool, mix with the oxtail and season. Moisten with a little stock and chill in the fridge.

Roll the pastry to 3mm thick and cut into 4 2-inch circles. Brush their rims with the beaten egg and fill with a tablespoon of oxtail. Fold over and seal the edge with a fork and brush with egg wash. Bake for 10 minutes in a medium oven gas mark 4 (180ºC).

For the sauce

Take 1 pint of the oxtail stock and boil until it is reduced to ¼ pint. Then add the beer and reduce until it becomes a light syrupy consistency. Season with salt and pepper.

For the steaks

Take the remaining shallot and sweat in the beef dripping, add the oatmeal and chopped sage leaves. Cook the mixture slowly for 5 minutes. Seal the steaks in a hot pan and then top with the oatmeal mixture. Finish the steaks in a medium to hot oven. The time will depend on how you like them but 7 minutes should give you a medium to rare steak. This will also depend on the thickness of the steak. Pan fry the mushrooms in a little olive oil and season.

To serve

Place the steaks on the middle of 4 warm plates, surround with the sauce, place an oxtail bridie on each plate and scatter the mushrooms around each steak. Serve with some buttered spinach.

Fillets of monkfish wrapped in pancetta, red pepper and caper sauce

Serves 4

Ingredients

2 large monkfish fillets
8 rashers pancetta
1 oz good quality small capers washed
2 shallots finely chopped
2 cloves wild garlic crushed
3 red peppers (deseeded and cut into chunks)
5 floz olive oil
5 floz water
2 large yellow courgettes
1 large green courgette
6 tomatoes (skinned, seeded and diced)
1 tbsp flat parsley
1 tbsp balsamic vinegar
1 tbsp basil (chopped)
Salt and pepper

"The best capers to look for are in brine or salt. Just rinse them lightly and they are ready to use. The smaller ones have more flavour and they give a bit of sharpness to th dish. Go to your deli for pancetta."

Method

For the monkfish, get your fish monger to trim the tails, you need four medallions cut from each tail weighing approximately 3oz each. Wrap the pancetta around the medallions and secure each with a cocktail stick.

For the sauce, put 2fl oz of oil in a pan and sweat the shallots, garlic and red peppers until soft. Then add the balsamic vinegar and the water and simmer for 15 minutes. Liquidise and strain. Adjust the seasoning and add the capers. Keep warm.

Cut the courgettes into small cubes. In a heavy frying pan, heat 2fl oz of the olive oil. Once the oil is hot, add the courgettes and fry until they colour but do not overcook. Add the herbs, tomatoes and then season.

Fry the monkfish quickly in the remaining 1fl oz of olive oil, making sure the oil is very hot, then finish the monkfish by placing in a medium oven gas mark 4 (180°C) for 6 minutes.

To serve, divide the warm courgette mix between 4 warm plates, place the monkfish on top and spoon pepper sauce around.

Langoustines in duck broth

Serves 4

Ingredients

2 duck carcasses for the stock
8 oz carrot diced
8 oz leeks diced
4 cloves garlic
2 onions diced
½ celery heads diced
4 pints water
20 langoustines
2 duck breasts
2 oz barley
5 oz leeks cut diagonally
3 oz finely diced carrot
2 oz finely diced courgettes
1 tbsp chopped chervil

Method

Roast the duck carcasses until brown in a hot oven. Sweat all the vegetables and garlic in a large pan and add the carcasses and cover with water. Bring to the boil and simmer for 3 hours. Strain and refrigerate.

Take 2 pints of the stock from the fridge. Skim the fat off the top. Bring to the boil and reduce until 1½ pints of rich duck broth remain. Blanch the langoustines in boiling water. Shell them and take the vein out of the back. Cook the barley in ½ pint of water.

You will need about 1½ pints of the rich duck broth seasoned and boiling. Add the barley first, then the vegetables. Simmer until tender and then add the langoustines. Season the duck breasts and pan fry until they are cooked pink.

Divide the langoustine and vegetable broth equally between 4 bowls. Sprinkle with chervil. Slice the duck and place into the broth.

"More adventurous gourmets may like to try this recipe with pigeon."

Bridget Hagmann

Glendale Salads

When Bridget Hagmann moved to Skye in 1983 she came further than most. Originally from Wiesbaden in Germany, she had visited Scotland many times and had set her heart on a croft.

She has become the main supplier of organic salad leaves, herbs and vegetables on Skye. She has won awards from the Soil Association in the mixed salad category and received commendations for her mixed herbs and courgettes. Her success is all the more astonishing considering her previous inexperience: "Before we moved we never even had a houseplant".

She bought a lot of books and acknowledges the help her neighbours gave her in pointing out the easiest growing plants. Bridget initially gave away her surplus but then started selling it to shops. Soon she realised that it was the same people coming again and again and she had a business on her hands.

One of the aspects of the job she most enjoys is showing chefs around and seeing what they get up to. "I do a lot of my own delivering and love going into the kitchens," she says. This is one of the reasons she tries to work closely with the chefs, like John Kelly, to try and provide what they want. She has a simple recipe for success. "I love to cook and so do my team."

Lightly curried John Dory on wilted courgette flowers

Serves 4

Ingredients
8 fillets of John Dory
1 tsp mild curry powder
2 tbsp olive oil
2 oz butter
16 courgette flowers
2 lb mussels
16 shitake mushrooms
6 tomatoes (peeled, seeded and chopped)
1 tbsp grain mustard
2 floz red wine vinegar
6 floz olive oil
1 tbsp chopped chives
1 tbsp chopped chervil
1 tsp chopped basil
Salt and pepper

"It is best to buy courgette flowers on the day you use them as they will wilt very quickly."

For the vinaigrette
Steam the mussels, shell and reserve in 1 tablespoon of oil. Pan fry the mushrooms then drain on kitchen paper. Pour the red wine vinegar into a bowl with the mustard and whisk in the 6 floz of olive oil. Add all the herbs, the chopped tomatoes, the mushrooms and the mussels.

For the John Dory
Lay them flat on a board, sprinkle with salt, pepper and curry powder. Heat a large frying pan and add 2 tbsp of olive oil. When the oil is hot add 1oz of butter then the fillets, skin side down. Turn them after 1 minute and cook until firm – usually 2 more minutes but this will depend on thickness of fillet.

For the flowers
Remove the base of the courgettes. Warm 1oz of butter until bubbling, add the flowers and wilt, then season.

To assemble
Divide the flowers between 4 warm plates, place 2 fillets on top of the flowers. Surround with the vinaigrette, splitting the mussels and mushrooms equally.

Pan seared loin of lamb on lentil casserole with buttered pak choi and wild garlic jus

Serves 4

Ingredients

4 5 oz lamb loin trimmed
2 lamb's kidneys
6 oz pak choi
I oz butter
4 oz lentils
2 dashes olive oil
4 oz streaky bacon
2 shallots diced
2 oz diced carrots
2 oz diced leeks
2 oz diced celeriac
I oz diced celery
I bouquet garni (thyme, bayleaf, parsley)
½ pt lamb stock
¼ pt red wine
2 finely diced shallots
10 floz lamb stock
10 floz wine
2 tbsp honey
I oz diced butter
sprig rosemary
3 cloves wild garlic (crushed and peeled)

Method

To make the lentil casserole, heat a heavy based pan, add a dash of olive oil and add the bacon until lightly browned. Add the vegetables and sweat for 2 minutes.

Then add the lentils, lamb stock and red wine. Bring to the boil then simmer with the bouquet garni for approximately 30 minutes until the lentils are soft.

For the sauce

Heat a saucepan, add a dash of olive oil and add the shallots and peeled crushed garlic cloves. Sweat for 3 minutes then add the stock, wine, honey and sprig of rosemary. Simmer the sauce until a light syrupy consistency is reached, strain, then whisk in the butter. Do not re-boil. Keep warm until needed.

For the meat

To prepare the kidneys, cut them in half and cut the centres out with a sharp knife. In a large frying pan, heat some olive oil and sauté the lamb until pink. Fry the kidneys, keeping them pink, and season with salt and pepper. Sauté the pak choi in a little butter

To assemble

Place the lentils in the middle of 4 warm plates. Top the lentils with the pak choi and the sliced lamb, garnish with the kidney and surround with the wild garlic sauce.

Poached halibut, smoked trout, baked beetroot and watercress sauce

Serves 4

Ingredients
I pt milk
4 6oz Halibut fillets
4 tbsp coarse salt
2 slices cold smoked trout
8 beetroot (uncooked) un-
peeled
2 tsp grain mustard
6 tbsp olive oil
I tbsp chopped fresh tarragon
4 floz dry white wine
10 floz fish stock
5 floz double cream
I oz butter
2 shallots finely chopped
Salt and pepper
Bunch of watercress

"Bear in mind that you don't want to overcook the watercress. Use a hand blender to foam up the sauce, as that gives it a frothiness and lightness."

For the beetroot

Drizzle 4 tbsp of olive oil over the beetroot on a tray and sprinkle with the coarse salt. Bake in their skins in a medium oven for 1 hour or until they are firm. Peel the beetroot, dice and mix the mustard, tarragon and a little olive oil with the beetroot and keep warm.

For the sauce

Melt the butter in a pan and sweat the shallots for a couple of minutes. Add the white wine and reduce by half.

Then add the fish stock and double cream and reduce until a high syrupy consistency is achieved. Cut the stalks off the watercress and wash, then dry and add to the sauce. Bring the sauce back to the boil and then liquidise and pass through a sieve. Check the consistency (it should be syrupy) and seasoning and keep warm.

To cook the halibut

Bring the milk to a simmer, cut the smoked trout into 4 long strips about 2 inches in diameter and wrap around the halibut. Place the halibut into the simmering milk for 3 minutes depending on thickness.

To assemble

Divide the beetroot between 4 warm plates, preferably in metal rings to keep a nice shape, drain the halibut on kitchen paper and place on the beetroot and surround with sauce.

Poached salmon in aromatic broth

Serves 4

Ingredients

4 6oz wild or organic salmon
fillets de-scaled
2 oz carrot ribbons
2 oz courgette ribbons
2 oz leek diced
2 oz small celery strips
½ small onion sliced
2½ pints fish stock
Sprig thyme
Sprig dill
4 star anise
1 bay leaf
5 floz white wine
1 measure Pernod
2 tbsp cream
1 oz butter
2 tbsp chives
12 oz baby vegetables

Method

Bring the stock, wine, star anise, onion, leeks, celery, herbs, bay leaf and Pernod to the boil and simmer for 15 minutes. Slide the salmon portions into the stock and simmer for 5 minutes. Take the salmon out and keep warm in a little stock.

Take half the stock out of the pan and reduce until it has a syrupy consistency. Add the cream, reduce further then whisk the 1oz of butter into the sauce and keep warm. Do not re-boil.

The poaching liquor can now be brought back to a simmer. Add the courgette and carrot ribbons, simmer for 2 minutes, remove and keep warm. Add the baby vegetables and simmer until tender then add the chives.

To serve, divide the vegetables between 4 pasta bowls place the salmon on top, separate the baby vegetables around each salmon with a little of the stock, and serve with the sauce in a sauce boat.

"When you are preparing this, you don't want your vegetables too crisp."

Roast turbot fillet and a broth of saffron mussels and clams

Serves 4

Ingredients

4 6oz turbot fillets
1 tbsp olive oil
1 lb potatoes for mashing
2 oz dry cure bacon
3 oz finely diced leeks
4 tbsp cream
Salt and pepper
16 mussels
16 surf clams
½ pint white wine
½ pint fish stock
2 shallots finely diced
1 tsp chopped chives
1 tsp chopped dill
1 pinch saffron strands
2 oz butter
2 floz cream

"We use surf clams but they are difficult to get. You can use poulardes, a larger clam, but you would only need half the amount for this recipe."

For the mash

Wash, peel and boil the potatoes until cooked. Drain and leave to dry. Sauté the bacon in 1oz butter until lightly brown, add the leeks and sweat for 1 minute, add the cream and reduce until thickened. Mash the potatoes and then beat the leek mix into it and season. Keep warm.

For the sauce

Steam the clams and mussels in white wine. When they have opened take them out and keep warm. Sieve the wine through a cloth and keep aside. Heat the 1oz butter, sweat the shallots, add the fish stock, the cooking wine and the cream and reduce until a light syrup consistency. Then add the herbs and season the shellfish.

To finish

Heat an ovenproof pan adding the oil when it is hot and the fillets of turbot. When they are a light golden colour turn and season. Place in a medium oven for up to 7 minutes, depending on thickness. Divide the mash between four warm pasta type bowls, place the fish on top and spoon the shellfish broth around using 4 mussels and 4 clams on each.

Neil Christie & Brigid Maclachlan

Lusta Fungi

It was a trip to Glastonbury and Green Gathering that piqued Neil Christie and Brigid Maclachlan's interest in mushrooms. The former rock and roller who had worked building stages for the music industry was intrigued by a display showing how to grow oyster mushrooms on toilet rolls.

By 2001, with the help and guidance of Humungus Fungus, Neil and his partner Brigid decided to go into production. Five years on, and with full Soil Association accreditation, they now supply restaurants on Skye with an array of mushrooms: shitake, grey and king oyster, lion's mane and maitake, all grown on oak sawdust with hardwood chips from a saw mill in Dumfriesshire.

What makes the fungi that Lusta supplies special is Neil and Brigid's absolute insistence on quality. "We are not under pressure to produce," says Neil.

The future brings continued growth. Neil talks of streamlining the business and diversifying into new varieties; compost-based mushrooms like morels. "We are easily selling everything," says Neil, adding the unavoidable pun: "Business is mushrooming."

Skye lobster poached in smoked paprika butter

Serves 4

Ingredients

4 Skye lobster
½ lb butter
5 floz water
I tbsp smoked paprika
½ lb cous cous
½ pint water
2 mangoes
I ½ oz butter
I ½ floz olive oil
I tsp ground cumin
I tsp Chinese spice
I tsp all spice
A little vegetable oil
6 tomatoes
I floz white wine vinegar
2½ floz olive oil
I tsp chopped basil

I tsp chopped coriander
Shells of 4 lobsters
5 oz shitake mushrooms
4 shallots
⅓ pint white wine
5 tomatoes
⅓ pint tomato juice
I measure brandy
I pint fish stock
I pint double cream
Juice of I lemon
2 cloves garlic

"This recipe was created by my sous chef James Dixon."

For the lobster

Place pot of water on stove, while putting the lobsters in the freezer for 10 minutes. Bring the water to boil, and have iced water at the ready. Place the lobster in boiling water for 2 minutes. Take out and put straight into iced water. When cool, take meat out of lobsters leaving the body and claws whole. Set aside in fridge.

For the sauce

Heat a pan on the stove. Add a few drops of vegetable oil and a knob of butter. Put in the shells, chopped tomatoes and shallots and fry off for 1 minute. Pour in the brandy and flame to burn off alcohol. Add white wine, fish stock, garlic and mushrooms and reduce by half, then add the tomato juice. Simmer on a low heat for 45 minutes. Take off the heat and pass through a sieve. Place the liquid into a pan and add the cream and lemon juice and bring to boil. Simmer until a good consistency is achieved. Season to taste and set aside.

For the tomatoes

Peel off the skin, de-seed the tomatoes and place on a dry, clean cloth and pat dry. Slice into strips. Pour the vinegar in a bowl, slowly add 2½ floz olive oil while whisking continuously. Put it in a pan and heat on the stove. Once hot, pour over the tomato slices and set aside. When they are cool add chopped basil and coriander and place in the fridge.

For the cous cous

Bring ½ pint of salted water to the boil in a pan, adding cumin, Chinese spice, all spice and the remaining olive oil. Take off the heat and pour into the cous cous stirring gently. Wrap in cling film and leave to fluff for 3 minutes. Add the butter and chopped mango and cook on a low heat turning frequently with a fork.

For the lobster

Pour 5 floz water and ½lb butter into small pot with the smoked paprika. Bring to the simmer. Turn down to a slow simmer add the lobster tail and claws. Cook for 4 minutes keeping the lobster in liquid. Take off the stove.

To assemble

Place the sauce back on the stove to heat. Place the cous cous in the mould pressing down. Take the tomatoes, drain them of all liquid in a sieve and place on top of the cous cous. Take the lobster from its poaching liquid. Place on a chopping board. Slice the body into 1cm thick pieces and neatly arrange on the tomatoes. Place the claws in the middle. Spoon the sauce around the plate. Garnish with a sprig of dill and coriander.

Venison loin with white beans in beer

Serves 4

Ingredients

4 6oz loins of venison
14 oz soaked white beans
4 oz streaky bacon (diced)
¾ oz olive oil
1 pint Black Cuillin beer
1 tbsp flour
2 shallots
2 oz diced carrots
2 oz diced leeks
2 oz diced celery
1 clove garlic (crushed)
1 bouquet garni (sprig thyme,
1 bay leaf, 2 parsley sprigs)
1 oz butter
6 juniper berries
Measure of gin
¾ pint game stock
1 tbsp vegetable oil
Buttered spring cabbage for
garnishing

"As with duck, you either have to cook venison pink or braise it for a long time. Anywhere in the middle and it just goes very tough. For loins it is best to keep them nice and pink."

Method

Heat the olive oil. First add the diced bacon, lightly brown, and then the beans and vegetables. Pour in the gin and flambé. Add the flour and the game stock, beer, garlic, berries, bouquet garni and simmer for 40 minutes until the beans are cooked.

Sauté the venison in the vegetable oil keeping it pink: slice and serve on the beans in a bowl or pasta plate accompanied by buttered spring cabbage.

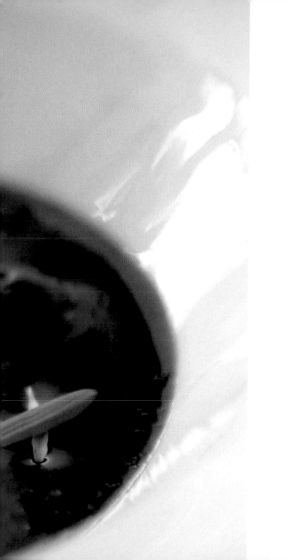

Blueberry and thyme soup with iced white chocolate fondant and praline biscuits

Desserts

Banana tart tatin

Serves 4

Ingredients
8 oz filo pastry
2 bananas
2 oz icing sugar
4 floz butterscotch sauce (see
recipe on page 106)
2 oz butter

Rum sorbet
1 pint water
14oz demerara sugar
double measure demerara
rum

Method
Set your oven to its highest temperature well in
advance.

For the sorbet
Place the water in a pot and bring to the boil. Add
the demerara sugar and simmer for 10 minutes.
Then add the rum, cool and churn in an ice cream
machine. If you don't have an ice cream machine,
freeze for 4 hours, stirring every half hour.

For the bananas
Take the filo pastry and cut out 8 banana shapes,
slightly larger than the bananas you have. Split and
sear the bananas in a very hot pan then cool quickly
by putting them in the freezer for 20 minutes. Butter
a shallow pan and brush with the butterscotch
sauce. Split the bananas lengthways and place them
cut side down in the pan. Dust with icing sugar and
place a sheet of pastry over each banana. Brush the
pastry with melted butter and then add another
sheet of pastry and dust with the icing sugar. Bake
in the very hot oven. (This should take about 4
minutes depending on your oven). Finish with some
butterscotch sauce and the rum sorbet.

Blueberry and thyme soup with iced white chocolate fondant and praline biscuits

Ingredients

White Chocolate Fondant
4 oz castor sugar
8 tbsp water
5 egg yolks
9 oz white chocolate
1 pint cream

Praline Biscuits
½ lb castor sugar
½ lb hazelnuts

Blueberry Soup
¾ lb blueberries
10 floz apple juice
2 oz castor sugar
2 sprigs thyme
1 apple (skinned and diced)

"This recipe will make more than you need in one sitting but you can easily keep it in the freezer for the next time you have friends round."

For the white chocolate fondant

Lightly whisk the cream and put into the fridge. Bring 4oz of the caster sugar and water to boil until syrup. Take off the heat. Add the warm syrup to the egg yolks in a large bowl and whisk over a pan of simmering water until the mixture turns pale. Add the white chocolate, and take off the heat. The chocolate will melt into the mixture. Fold the mixture into the whipped cream from the fridge and pour into moulds and freeze for 8 hours.

For the blueberry soup

Put all ingredients into a saucepan and bring to the boil. Simmer for 6 minutes and then liquidize and then pass through a sieve and cool.

For the praline biscuits

Melt the sugar slowly until it turns to caramel. Add the hazelnuts and turn out into parchment paper and cool. Break praline into pieces and put into a blender until it is a sand consistency.

Spoon a thin layer of praline mix on to parchment paper in the shape of a circle, place in a hot oven until it melts and starts to bubble. This will only take a couple of minutes. Remove from the oven then leave to cool down before removing from parchment paper.

Unmould the white chocolate. Place in 4 deep plates. Pour soup around the chocolate. Garnish with a biscuit.

Crowdie tart with pomegranate sauce

Serves 6

Ingredients

10 oz sweet pastry (see recipe on page 106)
1 stick of lemon grass
5 eggs
3½ oz castor sugar
10 fl oz cream
2½ oz flour
1 vanilla pod
7 oz crowdie
2 pomegranates
2 oz granulated sugar
1¼ floz grenadine
2 floz water

Method

Turn your oven on to gas mark 4 (180°C).

Roll out the sweet pastry and press in to the bottom of a 12" flan case and bake blind for 15 minutes.

Pound the stick of lemon grass on a board. Bring the cream, lemon grass and vanilla to the boil and then cool. Beat the egg with the castor sugar, add the flour and crowdie, add the cream and pour into the flan case and place in the oven for 20 minutes.

Bring the granulated sugar, water and grenadine to the boil and simmer until it reaches a syrupy consistency, add the pomegranate seeds, and boil for a further minute.

Once the tart cools, cut into portions and serve with pomegranate sauce.

"Crowdie is a cow's cheese a little like cottage cheese. In Scotland people used to make it at home in a pillow case. The texture is creamy, yet crumbly and it has a slightly sour taste."

Peter MacAskill

Loch Eishort Mussel Culture

It takes Peter MacAskill almost two years to grow mussels from the spat stage to being ready to eat. The ropes are set in mid-April, the perfect time of year for the shellfish. What gives them their unique, sweet taste is that they grow in Loch Eishort. "Mussels are filter feeders and as an inland loch, there is fresh water and some vegetable matter that has washed down from the hills," he explains.

As a former fisherman, MacAskill was a little sceptical when he started on a pilot scheme in 1987. "I thought it was ridiculous growing mussels on ropes," he says with a laugh, but he had encouraging results and grew more the following year. At the moment he produces between 60 and 80 tonnes per annum, most of which is sold throughout Skye and as far afield as Lochalsh.

"Skye shellfish used to go the continent or the big cities. Now people are looking for it here and they boast about it," he says. His initial scepticism gone, he is now evangelical about growing mussels on ropes. "They are not threatened by any predators," he says, "And they can feed 24 hours a day which allows for much tastier meat".

Fennel and aniseed cake with caramel oranges

Serves 6

Ingredients
10 floz water
5 oz castor sugar
2 star anise
1½ tsp cinnamon
1 clove
4 oranges
zest of 1 orange
4 eggs
8 oz castor sugar
10 oz self raising flour
8 oz butter
1 tbsp toasted fennel seeds

Method
Heat the oven to gas mark 3 (170°C).

Peel the oranges and cut into segments. Heat 5oz of the sugar in a heavy pan gently until it becomes a syrupy consistency and caramelises. Once the sugar is clear and light brown, take off the heat and cool. Once cooled down, add in the water and spices; bring to the boil and simmer until the sugar has dissolved, then pour over the oranges.

Beat the butter with the sugar, beat the eggs in slowly and then add the flour and the orange zest. Grind the fennel seeds and add them to the mix, then pour the mix into a lined cake tin and bake for 35 minutes.

Serve the cake warm with the orange segments and drizzle some of the syrup over the cake.

"You can grind the fennel seeds in a coffee grinder."

Fried porridge with raspberries and lemon cream
Serves 4

Ingredients
1¾ pint milk
3 oz porridge oats
2 oz cornflour
8 oz castor sugar
1 vanilla pod
1 cinnamon stick
1 strip of lemon zest
2 eggs
2 oz plain flour
8 oz raspberries
8 floz cream
Zest and juice of 1 lemon
Icing sugar for dusting

Method
Split the vanilla pod, and add to 1½ pints of the milk with the cinnamon stick and strip of lemon and bring to the boil. Sieve and put back into the pan with the porridge oats and simmer for 5 minutes. Mix the cornflour with the remaining milk and add to the mix with 7oz of sugar. Cook for a further 3 minutes and then pour onto a tray lined with greaseproof paper, chill for 4 hours in a fridge.

Beat the eggs and set aside. Then cut the porridge into 12 triangles, dip into the plain flour, then egg, then flour once again and fry in hot oil for 2 minutes each side. Whip the cream with the remaining sugar and add the lemon juice and zest.

Place 3 porridge triangles on a plate with a scoop of cream and raspberries and dust with icing sugar. Serve.

"The idea for this came from a really old French recipe in which a special type of cream cheese is set with cornflour before it is fried. The idea is a little like beignets. But, please, make sure you don't fry in olive oil. Best to shallow fry the triangles in clarified butter."

Heather honey and toasted oatmeal tart with mandarins and grapefruit in Cointreau

Serves 8

Ingredients

10oz sweet pastry (see recipe on page 104)
5 eggs
4floz double cream
6oz castor sugar
4floz honey
2oz tossed oatmeal
2 mandarins
1 grapefruit
Measure of Cointreau
1oz castor sugar

"This tart is best served once it cools down but has not been refrigerated."

Method

Heat oven to gas mark 4 (180°C). Press the sweet pastry in to a 12" pastry case and blind bake making sure there are no holes in it, as the liquid will leak through when cooking.

For the filling

Melt the 6oz castor sugar over a low heat until it becomes liquid. Take off the heat and cool slightly and then add the honey and cream. (Take care as the sugar may splatter, best to use rubber gloves and pour away from yourself).

Return to the cooker and bring the sugar mixture back to the boil until fully melted then take it off the heat and leave until warm. Whisk the eggs in a large bowl and pour the sugar mixture onto the eggs, add the oatmeal, pour into the pastry case and bake for 20 minutes.

Once the flan is ready, leave to cool for 4 hours before cutting.

For the mandarins and grapefruit

Segment the fruit with a sharp knife, making sure there is no pith on the segments . Do this over a bowl and catch all the juice. Place the juice in a pan with the Cointreau and 1oz sugar and reduce by half, then pour over the segments.

To present

Serve the tart on chilled plates with the segments and a little of the juice drizzled around the tart

Jellied wee drams
Serves 4

Ingredients
2½ floz whisky (preferably single malt)
2½ floz sweet white wine
5 floz soda water
1 oz sugar
2 leaves gelatine
2 oz blueberries
2 oz raspberries
2 oz strawberries
3 oz sugar
5 floz water
piece of lemon peel
3 tbsp water
8 oz plain flour
2 oz icing sugar
8 oz butter
2 oz castor sugar
4 oz cornflour
Castor sugar to dust
Sprigs of mint

"Add the soda water just before the cooled liquid turns to jelly and you will capture some of the bubbles in the jelly. The shortbread mix will make more than you need, but can be stored in an airtight container."

Method
Bring the 5floz water and 3oz of sugar to the boil and simmer until it reaches a syrupy consistency. Add the lemon peel and the berries. Leave to cool and refrigerate.

For the shortbread mix
Preheat the oven to gas mark 3 (170°C). Cream the castor sugar, icing sugar and butter then add the plain flour and cornflour, and then rub in the butter. The mix will come together to form a dough. Roll out to about 4 mm and cut into disks. (You will need 8). Place on a baking tray and bake for 15 minutes. When ready cool on a rack and dust with castor sugar.

For the jellies
Soak the gelatine in 3 tbsp water and bring the wine, whisky and sugar to the boil. Squeeze the water from the gelatine and add to the whisky. Cool the mixture but not until it sets. Add the soda water and then pour into moulds. (Espresso cups are quite good as moulds). Leave to set in the fridge – this will take up to 6 hours.

To present
Un-mould the jellies and place in the middle of a cold sweet bowl, spoon the berries around, top with a sprig of mint and serve with the shortbread.

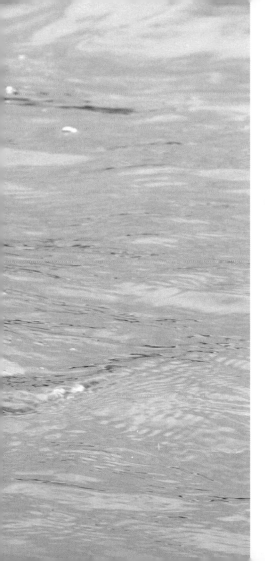

David Oakes

Oakes Marine

A professional diver for most of his life, work brought David to Skye in 1986 and two years later he started cultivating scallops, or ranching as professionals prefer to call it.

"It has been a steep learning curve," he admits, "and hard work to become a success". But the quality of his scallops has won out in the end.

It is a long process. Initially he keeps his scallops in lanterns as protection. In that kind of monoculture, they have the time they need to grow. After two years or so, when they are robust enough to avoid hungry predators like starfish and crabs, they get put on the sea bed.

In the early years, he sold virtually all of his produce to France although homegrown demand has seen that change. "Most of my scallops now stay on the island," he says, with a nod to Skye's growing international reputation for excellence in seafood dining. "If you are a restaurant that doesn't supply local produce, you change hands. People will pay for freshness, a taste of the island."

Lemon and basil tart

Serves 8

Ingredients
4 lemons
8oz castor sugar
6 eggs
½ pint cream
1 bunch of basil
1 blind baked sweet pastry
case (12-inch diameter)

Method
Set your oven to gas mark 2 (150°C). Grate the
lemon zest and keep separate. Juice the lemons and
place in a pan with the basil and sugar. Bring to the
boil and leave to infuse for 2 hours then strain.

Whisk the eggs and cream into the liquid. Pour
the mixture into the pastry case and bake for 40
minutes at gas mark 2. Leave to set for 2 hours
before cutting. Serve with basil or rhubarb sorbet.
(see recipe on page 106).

Warm lavender chocolate cake with cardamom spiced rhubarb compote and lavender cream

Serves 6

Ingredients
12oz dark chocolate
2 sprigs of lavender
4 eggs
4oz castor sugar
2 stalks of rhubarb
6 cardamom seeds
4 oz castor sugar
6 floz water
6 floz double cream
1oz castor sugar
1 sprig lavender

"In this recipe we use finely chopped fresh lavender but dried works just as well."

Method
Preheat the oven to gas mark 6 (200°C). Separate the eggs. Melt the chocolate and add the egg yolks and finely chopped lavender. Whisk the egg whites with the sugar until it forms peaks and fold into the chocolate mixture. Put the mixture into buttered ramekin dishes and then bake in the oven for 12 minutes. Leave to cool and set for about 15 minutes before un-moulding.

Slice the rhubarb at an angle. Bring the water and 4oz castor sugar to boil with cardamom seeds and simmer for 10 minutes then add the sliced rhubarb and take off the cooker. Allow to cool.

Chop the lavender finely. Whip the cream until it forms peaks. Add the 1oz castor sugar and lavender to the cream.

To assemble
Place a chocolate cake in the middle of each plate, surround with rhubarb compote, place a quenelle of lavender cream on top of the cake then a sprig of lavender.

Warm Skye beer and date cake

Serves 4

Ingredients

Beer Ice Cream
4 oz castor sugar
6 tbsp water
6 egg yolks
10 floz double cream
1 vanilla pod
8 floz beer (Red Cuillin)

Date cake
½ pint Red Cuillin beer
6 oz dates
2 oz butter
6 oz castor sugar
3 eggs
½ tsp bicarbonate of soda
6 oz self raising flower
2 tsp sesame seeds

"We have a commercial ice cream maker, but there is not much difference in flavour or texture between ours and what you can make with a domestic maker."

For the ice cream

Bring the castor sugar and water to the boil and simmer until a syrupy consistency, cool down. Bring the cream to the boil with the split vanilla pod. Meanwhile, whisk the yolks with the warm syrup until they turn pale and then add the beer.

Pour the hot cream onto the yolks. Continue whisking, then pour the mixture into a heavy base pan and stir over a low heat with a wooden spoon until the mixture coats the back of the spoon. Sieve the mixture and cool quickly. When cool, churn in an ice cream machine.

For the cake

Bring the dates and the beer to the boil. Take off the heat and add the bicarbonate of soda and leave to cool. Cream the sugar with the butter. Slowly add the eggs and then the flour – finally folding in the date mixture. Put into a lined baking tin, sprinkle with sesame seeds and bake on gas mark 4 (180ºC) for 40 minutes or until cooked.

Serve with butterscotch sauce (see recipe on page 106).

Stocks & Sorbets

Mint and Vanilla Sorbet
1 pint water
6 oz castor sugar
2 vanilla pods
2 drops spearmint
Split the vanilla. Scrape the seeds into a pan with the pods. Add the water, sugar and vanilla. Boil rapidly for 8 minutes. Leave to cool then strain. Churn in an ice cream machine until set or freeze for 4 hours, stirring every half hour.

Basil Sorbet
1 pint water
6 oz castor sugar
Large bunch of fresh basil
Bring the sugar and water to the boil. Add the basil and simmer for 8 minutes. Cool with the basil still in the syrup then strain. Churn in an ice cream machine or freeze for 4 hours, stirring every half hour.

Rhubarb Sorbet
1 pint water
7 oz castor sugar
12 oz rhubarb
Slice the rhubarb. Put the sugar and the rhubarb in a pan and heat slowly until the rhubarb completely softens, then pass through a sieve. Bring the remaining sugar and water to the boil and simmer for 8 minutes. Once cool, add the rhubarb puree and churn in an ice cream machine or freeze for 4 hours, stirring every half hour.

Butterscotch Sauce
4 oz soft brown sugar
4 oz syrup
4 oz butter
2 floz double cream
Bring the soft brown sugar, butter and syrup to the boil then let it simmer until the sugar is completely dissolved. Mix in the cream and take off the heat.

Sweet Pastry
8 oz butter
4 oz castor sugar
1 egg
14 oz plain flour
Pinch of salt
A drop of water
Cream the butter and sugar together and slowly beat in the egg. Mix in the flour and salt until you have a smooth mixture. Work the mixture into a ball and rest in the fridge until it is needed.

Pasta Dough
10 oz flour
2 whole eggs
2 egg yolks
2 tbsp finely chopped herbs (chervil, parsley, dill)
Pinch of salt
Blitz all the ingredients together in a food processor until it comes together like breadcrumbs. Take it out of the processor and knead until it comes

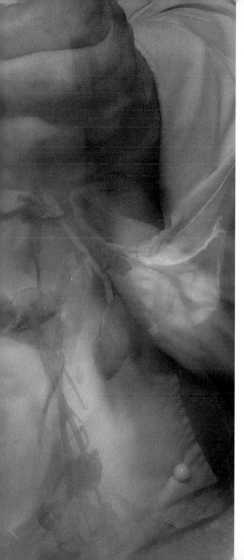

together like a dough. Wrap and refrigerate until you need to roll out.

Basic Fish Stock
makes 1½ pints
1 tbsp olive oil
2lb fish bones
2 pints cold water
2oz diced onion (roughly chopped)
4oz carrot (roughly chopped)
4oz leek (roughly chopped)
1 stick celery (roughly chopped)
1 bay leaf
½ pint white wine
1 fennel bulb diced
sprigs of thyme dill and parsley

Wash the fish bones and chop roughly. Sweat all the vegetables in a deep pan with olive oil. Add all the rest of the ingredients and simmer slowly for 20 minutes. Leave off the heat for an hour, then pass through a fine sieve. Chill until needed.

Never cook fish stock for longer than 20 minutes. If you do, the bones make the stock bitter and it tastes horrible. But once you have sieved out the bones you can reduce it down as much as you like.

Quick Meat Stock (Chicken, Beef, Duck, Lamb, Game)
makes 4 pints
4½ lb bones roughly chopped
8 pints cold water
2 onions chopped
2 leeks chopped
4 carrots chopped
4 celery sticks chopped
sprig of thyme
parsley stalks
8 peppercorns
6 cloves garlic

Roast the bones and vegetables and drain of oil, then place in a pan. Cover with water, add the herbs and peppercorns, then bring to the boil and turn down to simmer for 3 hours, skimming every half an hour. Remove from the heat and leave to cool. Strain whilst warm and refrigerate.

The trick to keeping your stock clear is to simmer it as gently as possible. Just bring it to the boil quickly and then let it bubble really slowly. The other trick is not to add anything too starchy. Carrots, onions and celery are fine, but anything like parsnips or celeriac will make the stock cloudy.